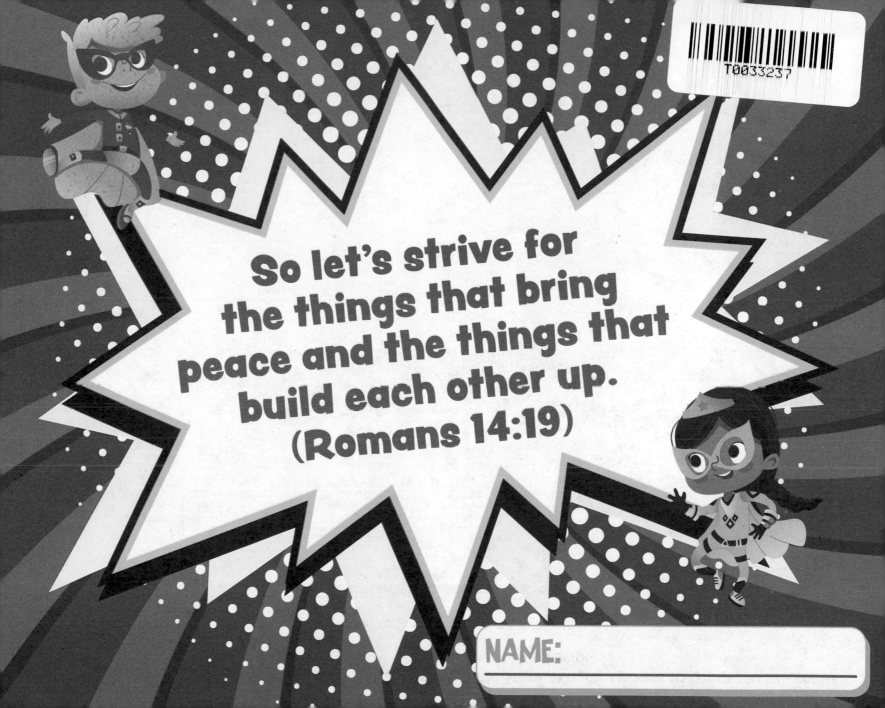

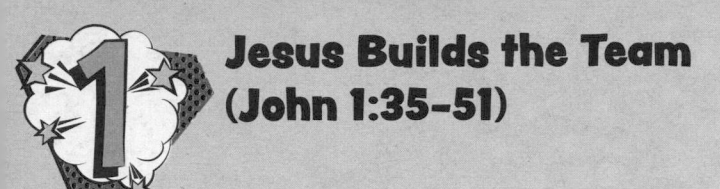

Jesus Builds the Team
(John 1:35-51)

Use the Bible Story Activity stickers to complete the scene. Can you count the disciples?

Hero Hotline

So let's strive for the things that bring peace and the things that build each other up. (Romans 14:19)

At Hero Hotline, we are working together to answer God's call and serve others. Trace the lines from the phones to Super-Meer and help him answer the call!

Jesus asked his disciples to follow him. Help the disciples
follow the path to get to Jesus. Color the page.

Hero Hotline

So let's strive for the things that bring peace and the things that build each other up. (Romans 14:19)

Connect the dots to complete the picture. Repeat and color the Hotline Verse. Work with a friend to say the verse together!

So let's strive for the things that bring peace and the things that build each other up. Romans (14:19)

Heroes are called to help others! Circle the pictures that show someone helping another person.

3 Jethro Mentors Moses (Exodus 18)

Use the Bible Activity Stickers to complete the scene.

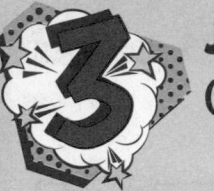

Hero Hotline

So let's strive for the things that bring peace and the things that build each other up. (Romans 14:19)

Can you find the hero cape that matches the hero mask?
Color the matching cape and mask the same color.

Hotline Tip
Heroes are called to Work Together!

Jethro encouraged Moses to find people to help him do God's work. Can you find and circle all of the objects that don't belong in the picture?

The Magnificent Magi
(Matthew 2:1-12)

Use the Bible Activity Stickers to complete the scene.

Hero Hotline

So let's strive for the things that bring peace and the things that build each other up. (Romans 14:19)

Heroes are called to listen to God! We can listen with our ears. Circle all the objects that make a sound.

Hotline Tip

Heroes are called to Listen to God!

The magi followed the star and listened to God. Can you find all the shapes in the picture below? Color the shapes.

5 Unexpected Heroes Give Paul a Basket Ride (Acts 9:1-25)

Use the Bible Activity Stickers to complete the scene.

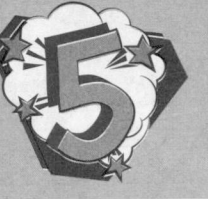

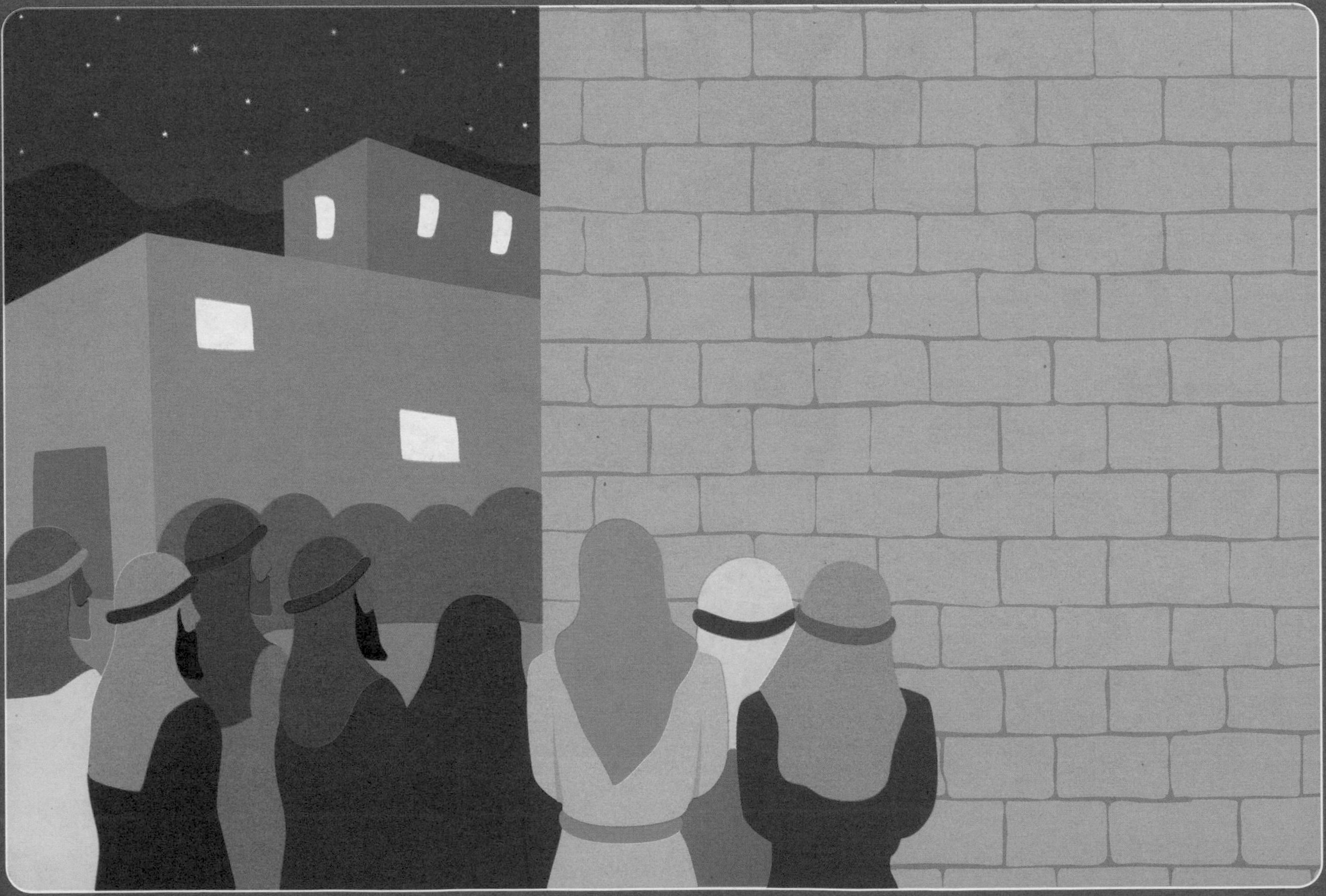

Hero Hotline

So let's strive for the things that bring peace and the things that build each other up. (Romans 14:19)

Color the picture of Super-Meer. Count all the superhero symbols in the picture.

Hotline Tip

Heroes are called to Show Grace!

Complete the picture by coloring or decorating the word Grace. How can you show grace to others?

GRACE